North American
Animals

COYOTES

by Joanne Mattern

Consulting Editor: Gail Saunders-Smith, PhD

CAPSTONE PRESS
a capstone imprint

Pebble Plus is published by Capstone Press,
1710 Roe Crest Drive, North Mankato, Minnesota 56003.
www.capstonepub.com

Library of Congress Cataloging-in-Publication Data
Mattern, Joanne, 1963–
    Coyotes / by Joanne Mattern.
        p. cm.—(Pebble plus. North American animals)
    Includes bibliographical references and index.
    Summary: "Simple text and full-color photographs provide a brief introduction to coyotes"—Provided by publisher.
    ISBN 978-1-4296-7700-4 (library binding)
    ISBN 978-1-4296-7923-7 (paperback)
    1. Coyote—Juvenile literature. I. Title.
    QL737.C22.M36476 2012
    599.7725—dc23   2011025690

Editorial Credits

Erika L. Shores, editor; Heidi Thompson, designer; Svetlana Zhurkin, media researcher;
    Kathy McColley, production specialist

Photo Credits

Creatas, cover; Dreamstime: Jim Kruger, 19, John James Henderson, 13, Reinhardt, 8–9, Rinus Baak, 15; iStockphoto:
Bev McConnell, 21, John Henderson, 5; Shutterstock: Blue Ice, 10–11; Shutterstock: Dennis Donohue, 7,
Richard Seeley, 16–17, Robert Kelsey, 1

Note to Parents and Teachers

The North American Animals series supports national science standards related to life science.
This book describes and illustrates coyotes. The images support early readers in understanding
the text. The repetition of words and phrases helps early readers learn new words. This book
also introduces early readers to subject-specific vocabulary words, which are defined in the
Glossary section. Early readers may need assistance to read some words and to use the Table of
Contents, Glossary, Read More, Internet Sites, and Index sections of the book.

Printed in the United States of America in North Mankato, Minnesota.
102011   006405CGS12

Table of Contents

Living in North America

A howl fills the air.

It's a coyote, calling to its pack.

All across North America,

people hear the howls of coyotes.

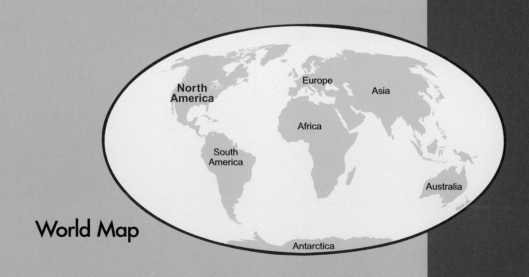

World Map

Coyotes live on North America's grasslands and deserts. They also live near people. Coyotes make their homes wherever they can find food.

North America Map

where coyotes live

Up Close!

Coyotes look like medium-size dogs. They weigh up to 50 pounds (23 kilograms). Large pointed ears and a long nose help coyotes find prey.

Coyotes have brown, gray, or red fur. Their chests and undersides are cream. Their bushy tails have a black tip.

Eating

Coyotes hunt mice, rabbits,
birds, and other small animals.
Most of the time, coyotes hunt
at night.

Coyotes are scavengers.
They eat dead animals
and garbage. Coyotes live
in so many places because
they'll eat almost anything.

Growing Up

In a pack, only the male
and female leaders mate.
Coyotes mate during winter.
Pups are born two months
after mating.

A female coyote usually has

a litter of six pups at a time.

Pups are born blind and helpless.

At 3 weeks old, pups play

outside the den.

Pack members teach pups
to hunt and howl.
At 6 to 8 months, coyotes can
leave the pack. They'll look
for mates and start new packs.

Glossary

den—a place where a wild animal lives; a female coyote gives birth to pups and keeps them safe in a den

howl—to make a loud, sad noise

mate—to join together to produce young; a mate is also the male or female partner of a pair of animals

pack—a small group of animals that lives and hunts together; some coyotes live in packs while others live alone

prey—an animal hunted by another animal for food

scavenger—an animal that looks through waste for food

Read More

Green, Emily. *Coyotes.* Backyard Wildlife. Minneapolis: Bellwether Media, 2011.

Lunis, Natalie. *Coyote: The Barking Dog.* Animal Loudmouths. New York: Bearport Pub., 2012.

Macken, JoAnn Early. *Coyotes.* Animals that Live in the Desert. Pleasantville, N.Y.: Weekly Reader, 2010.

Internet Sites

FactHound offers a safe, fun way to find Internet sites related to this book. All of the sites on FactHound have been researched by our staff.

Here's all you do:

Visit *www.facthound.com*

Type in this code: 9781429677004

Super-cool stuff! Check out projects, games and lots more at **www.capstonekids.com**

Index

Word Count: 200

Grade: 1

Early-Intervention Level: 19